The Ten Rules of the Modern Startup Founder

Table of Contents

Introduction: The Startup Revolution

- Understanding the Modern Startup Ecosystem
- Why These Rules Matter
- Who This Book is For
- Overview of the Journey Ahead

Part 1: Laying the Foundation

Rule #1: Vision Before Everything

- Defining a Clear Vision
- Balancing Passion with Pragmatism
- Visionaries Who Changed the Game

Rule #2: Customer Obsession is Key

- Building Products People Actually Want
- How to Truly Understand Your Target Market
- Gathering and Implementing Feedback Early

Rule #3: Build a Team, Not a Workforce

- Recruiting Passionate Talent
- Fostering a Strong Company Culture
- The Power of Diversity in Teams

Part 2: The Growth Phase

Rule #4: Fail Fast, Learn Faster

- Embracing Failure as Part of Growth
- Lean Methodologies & Iteration Cycles
- Case Studies of Startups that Learned from Failure

Rule #5: Master the Art of Networking

- Building Strategic Relationships
- Finding Mentors and Advisors
- The Role of Networking in Securing Funding

Rule #6: Be Financially Savvy

- Managing Cash Flow and Burn Rate
- Bootstrapping vs. Seeking Investment
- Navigating Seed Funding, Angel Investors, and VCs

Part 3: Scaling and Sustainability

Rule #7: Innovate Relentlessly

- How to Foster Continuous Innovation
- Staying Ahead in a Competitive Market
- Examples of Startups Leading in Innovation

Rule #8: Adapt or Die

- Navigating Market Shifts and Trends
- Pivoting Without Losing Your Core Identity
- Lessons from Startups that Adapted Successfully

Rule #9: Keep Your Customers Close

- Building Long-Term Customer Relationships
- Customer Retention Strategies
- Measuring and Improving Customer Satisfaction

Part 4: The Future of the Modern Startup

Rule #10: Lead with Purpose

- Defining Your Mission Beyond Profit
- The Role of Startups in Social Impact
- Why Purpose-Driven Companies Outlast the Rest

Conclusion: Your Journey as a Modern Founder

- Recap of the Ten Rules
- The Next Steps in Building Your Startup
- Staying Resilient and Focused

Acknowledgments
About the Author
Index

This structure ensures a comprehensive exploration of the key aspects of startup leadership, with actionable insights for founders at every stage of their journey.

Introduction: The Startup Revolution

Welcome, future startup moguls, hopeful dreamers, and those who just bought this book because the cover looked cool! You're about to dive into the wild, unpredictable, and often absurd world of startups. This isn't your average business book with jargon so thick you'd need a machete to cut through it. No, this is a comedic (yet oddly insightful) guide to navigating the crazy startup ecosystem. So, buckle up—this ride is going to have some steep drops, unexpected turns, and maybe even a few loop-de-loops. Let's get started, shall we?

Understanding the Modern Startup Ecosystem

Imagine you're at a party. Not just any party, but a Silicon Valley mixer. There are groups of people discussing blockchain, AI, and how their app is going to disrupt the coffee industry by connecting beans with end-users via a revolutionary peer-to-peer network. Welcome to the modern startup ecosystem, where everyone is a visionary, every coffee shop is a co-working space, and no one actually knows what "synergy" means but they use it anyway.

The startup ecosystem is a weirdly fascinating place where you'll find things like:

- Founders who haven't slept in three days because they're "hustling."
- Investors who pretend they know the difference between your AI-driven algorithm and a regular Google search.
- Coffee shops filled with people who look like they're coding but are probably just scrolling Twitter.

You see, startups have evolved from the days of a couple of college dropouts building computers in a garage. Today, it's all about apps, platforms, and "disrupting" whatever industry you can think of. Startups want to disrupt everything—transportation, food delivery, how we date, how we sleep, and probably how we breathe (just wait for the "Uber for Air" app). The key players in this ecosystem are not just the companies themselves but also the venture capitalists (VCs) who throw money at these ideas in the hopes of hitting the next big jackpot.

Why is this ecosystem so unique, you ask? It's like a giant petri dish where ideas can grow into billion-dollar enterprises or fizzle out faster than you can say "Series A." This is a world where failure is not just an option, it's practically a rite of passage. In fact, if you haven't failed at least once, some might argue you're not a real entrepreneur. It's a place where the only constant is change, and the only certainty is uncertainty.

Why These Rules Matter

Now, you might be wondering, "Why do I need rules in a world that seems to thrive on chaos?" Great question! You get a gold star for that one. The truth is, the startup ecosystem may look like a free-for-all, but there's an art (and a science) to surviving it. Imagine playing Monopoly, but instead of a board and dice, you have an Excel spreadsheet and a pitch deck. And every turn, a mysterious figure called "The Market" changes the rules without warning.

These rules matter because, while the startup world celebrates failure, we'd like to avoid it if possible. Sure, you learn a lot from failing, like the fact that you should never name your app something that sounds like a medical condition (RIP, "Quoravirus"). But wouldn't it be nice to succeed once in a while, maybe even build something that lasts longer than a flash-in-the-pan trend? That's where these rules come in.

The rules in this book are not some mystical commandments handed down by the startup gods. They're hard-earned lessons, learned by those who have been through the wringer and come out the other side (mostly) intact. Think of them as your survival guide to the jungle that is the modern startup world. These rules can help you navigate the pitfalls, dodge the traps, and maybe, just maybe, come out on top.

Who This Book Is For

So, who exactly is this book for? Good question, I'm glad you asked!

- **Aspiring Entrepreneurs:** If you have a million-dollar idea but no clue how to turn it into a business, this book is your new best friend.
- **Current Startup Founders:** If you're already in the thick of it and feel like you're herding cats while riding a unicycle, you'll find solace and guidance in these pages.
- **Startup Employees:** If you've ever wondered why your boss spends half the day on "strategy sessions" (read: brainstorming while playing ping pong), this book will give you some insights.
- **Venture Capitalists:** Yes, even you high-rollers can learn a thing or two. Plus, it'll help you understand what on earth those founders are talking about during pitches.
- **Curious Bystanders:** If you've ever looked at a startup and thought, "I could do that," but then immediately went back to your 9-to-5, this book is for you too. Consider it your starter kit for contemplating the plunge.

In short, this book is for anyone who's interested in startups, whether you're knee-deep in your own venture or just dipping your toes in the waters. It's also for people who enjoy a good laugh while learning valuable lessons. Because let's face it—startups are weird, wonderful, and often hilarious in their unpredictability.

Overview of the Journey Ahead

Now that we've got the introductions out of the way, let's talk about the journey ahead. This book is structured around ten rules that every modern startup founder should know. Think of them as your roadmap through the startup wilderness. Here's a sneak peek at what's to come:

1. **Vision Before Everything:** Before you do anything, you need a vision. Something that drives you and gives you a reason to wake up in the morning, even when your codebase is crashing and your coffee machine is broken.
2. **Customer Obsession is Key:** Spoiler alert: your startup isn't about you, it's about your customers. We'll delve into how to make them love you (or at least tolerate you).
3. **Build a Team, Not a Workforce:** Learn why hiring your cousin's roommate's dog-walker because they're "cheap" is not a great idea.
4. **Fail Fast, Learn Faster:** The faster you fail, the quicker you learn. And in the startup world, learning quickly can be the difference between success and becoming a cautionary tale.
5. **Master the Art of Networking:** You're only as good as your network. And yes, that means more LinkedIn messages.

1. **Be Financially Savvy:** It's all fun and games until you run out of money. We'll cover how to keep your finances in check without selling a kidney.
2. **Innovate Relentlessly:** You can't rest on your laurels. Mainly because laurels don't pay the bills.
3. **Adapt or Die:** If you can't change with the times, the times will change you. And not in a good way.
4. **Keep Your Customers Close:** A happy customer is a repeat customer. And a repeat customer is… well, you get the point.
5. **Lead with Purpose:** At the end of the day, what's your startup's reason for existing? If it's just to make a quick buck, you might be in the wrong game.

Each of these rules comes with its own set of challenges, nuances, and, of course, humorous anecdotes. By the end of this book, you'll have a clearer understanding of what it takes to be a modern startup founder. You'll also have a few laughs along the way, which is crucial because if you can't laugh at the absurdity of it all, you're in for a rough ride.

So, grab a cup of coffee (or a kale smoothie if that's your thing) and get comfortable. The startup revolution is in full swing, and you're about to become a part of it. Whether you're building the next unicorn or just trying to make it through the next pitch meeting, this book is here to guide, inspire, and entertain you.

Let's start this revolution, shall we?

Rule # 1: Vision Before Everything

Let's face it: if you're launching a startup in today's world, you're either a bold visionary, an adrenaline junkie, or completely out of your mind. Maybe all three! In any case, there's one thing we know for sure: **vision** is the make-or-break element for any startup founder. It's the invisible force that propels your wild idea from late-night scribbles on a napkin to a pitch deck in front of venture capitalists, who nod politely while secretly wondering how much longer they have to listen before they can say, "We're going to pass."

But what exactly is vision? No, it's not just a flowery term that tech bros like to throw around to sound deep at networking events. Vision is **the why** behind your startup. Why are you subjecting yourself to sleepless nights, cold sweat, and an unhealthy amount of caffeine? What are you hoping to achieve? In this chapter, we'll explore how to define a clear vision, why balancing passion with pragmatism is crucial, and dive into the stories of some visionaries who changed the game (and made it look way easier than it actually is).

Defining a Clear Vision

So you've decided to start a company. Maybe you were tired of working a 9-to-5. Maybe you had a dream (literally) about a new kind of toilet paper, or perhaps you were inspired by all the motivational memes flooding your Instagram feed. Either way, you're here now, staring at a blank page (or screen) trying to figure out what the heck your startup is supposed to do.

Vision is like your startup's GPS. Without it, you're just driving around aimlessly, getting increasingly frustrated, and probably running out of gas. So, let's get started by defining what a clear vision looks like.

The Magic Formula for Vision

Contrary to popular belief, a clear vision is not just a vague, feel-good statement like, "We're going to change the world!" (That's great, but how? Are you delivering pizza via drones, curing cancer, or inventing biodegradable coffee cups that disintegrate once they leave your hand?) A real vision needs **direction**.

Here's the magic formula for a killer vision statement:

Vision = The What + The Why + The Wow

- **The What**: What is your product or service? Be as specific as possible. For example, "We provide wearable tech for dogs."
- **The Why**: Why does this matter? How is it solving a problem that people genuinely care about? ("Because all dogs should be able to track their steps and calories, obviously.")
- **The Wow**: What's the big impact? How will the world be different because of your genius? ("We're creating a healthier, happier canine society with fewer lazy Labradors.")

Put it together, and you've got something like this:

"Our vision is to revolutionize pet health by creating innovative, wearable tech that helps dogs live longer, healthier lives."

Boom! Now you're no longer just "making dog Fitbits," you're a visionary who's ***revolutionizing*** the world of pet health. Go ahead, take a moment to let that sink in. Feels good, doesn't it?

Vision Quest: Find Yours

If you're still struggling to come up with a vision, don't worry. You're not alone. Even the greatest founders had moments where they weren't sure what they were doing. (Legend has it that Steve Jobs once contemplated opening a fruit stand. Ok, that's not true, but can you blame me for imagining it?)

Start by asking yourself these three key questions:

What problem am I solving?

If your startup isn't solving a problem, then what's the point? Your vision should address a real need, not just something you think is cool.

Why am I the right person to solve it?

Spoiler alert: if you're creating an app that connects rock-climbing hamsters but you're afraid of heights and allergic to rodents, you might want to reconsider.

What's my dream scenario in 10 years?

Picture your startup in the future. What does success look like? If your answer involves flying private jets and sipping champagne on a yacht, cool, but that's not a vision. Think bigger—how will your company actually change things?

Once you have your answers, congratulations—you now have a vision. It may not be perfect, but guess what? That's OK. Visions evolve, just like your company will (hopefully). Now, let's move on to something equally important: **balancing passion with pragmatism**.

Balancing Passion with Pragmatism

Ah, passion. It's the lifeblood of startups, the fiery enthusiasm that makes you work 80 hours a week for a company that still exists only on paper. Passion is what gets you up in the morning (that and the realization that you've burned through most of your savings and can't afford to fail). It's the thing that makes you believe that your gluten-free, eco-friendly, solar-powered waffle maker is going to change breakfast forever.

But here's the kicker: **passion alone isn't enough**. Passion, when left unchecked, can lead you straight into a delusional land where every idea you have is brilliant and the only reason it's not working is because "people just don't get it yet."

Enter **pragmatism**. Pragmatism is passion's less sexy but incredibly necessary sibling. It's the voice of reason that whispers, "Hey, maybe we should test this idea before we spend all our money on it," or "Perhaps no one needs an app that helps you match your socks." Pragmatism keeps you grounded, ensures you make decisions based on reality, and saves you from becoming *that* founder—the one everyone avoids at conferences because they've heard your elevator pitch 37 times and still don't know what your company does.

Passion and Pragmatism: The Odd Couple

Here's the thing: passion and pragmatism aren't enemies. In fact, they're the ultimate power couple (think Beyoncé and Jay-Z, but for startups). Passion is what drives you forward; pragmatism is what makes sure you're not driving off a cliff.

The key is finding balance. Too much passion, and you'll end up wasting time and resources on things that don't work. Too much pragmatism, and you'll never take risks or try anything bold. To strike the perfect balance, follow these guidelines:

1. **Test before you invest**: Passion will make you want to dive headfirst into your idea. Pragmatism will remind you that diving without checking the water depth is a terrible plan. Test your idea with a small audience before going all-in.
2. **Accept feedback (even when it hurts)**: Passionate founders can be defensive about their ideas. But here's the harsh truth: sometimes your baby is ugly. Pragmatism means listening to feedback and adjusting your approach, even if it stings.
3. **Have a plan (but be ready to pivot)**: Passion wants you to believe that your original idea is perfect and nothing needs to change. Pragmatism knows that flexibility is key to survival. Have a plan, but don't be afraid to pivot if things aren't working.

1. **Keep your ego in check**: Passion can make you think you're the next Steve Jobs. Pragmatism will remind you that you're not (yet). Confidence is important, but humility will help you learn, grow, and ultimately succeed.

By balancing passion with pragmatism, you'll be able to make smart decisions without losing the fire that made you start your company in the first place. Now, let's take a look at some **visionaries who changed the game**.

Visionaries Who Changed the Game

No book on vision would be complete without a look at the people who took their wild ideas and turned them into something extraordinary. These founders had vision, sure—but they also knew how to balance passion with pragmatism (and, occasionally, a touch of madness).

1. Elon Musk: The Martian Dreamer

Love him or hate him, there's no denying that Elon Musk has vision (and plenty of it). The man wants to colonize Mars, after all. Musk's vision for SpaceX wasn't just about building rockets—it was about making humans an interplanetary species. Lofty, right? But here's where the pragmatism comes in: Musk didn't just daydream about space travel, he focused on making space exploration cheaper and more efficient, with a step-by-step plan to get there. He used passion to dream big and pragmatism to figure out how to make that dream a reality. (Bonus points for managing to launch a car into space just for fun.)

2. Sara Blakely: The Underdog

Sara Blakely, the founder of Spanx, didn't just create a product—she solved a problem that countless women didn't even know they had: uncomfortable undergarments. Blakely's vision was clear: to help women feel confident and comfortable. But she didn't stop there. Armed with $5,000 in savings and zero experience in fashion, she used sheer tenacity (passion) and clever strategy (pragmatism) to turn Spanx into a billion-dollar company. Her story proves that you don't need to be a tech genius to have vision—sometimes, you just need to know how to make people's lives a little better (and maybe a little less pinchy).

3. Jeff Bezos: The Long Game Player

Before Jeff Bezos was the richest man on the planet, he was just a guy selling books out of his garage. But Bezos had a vision far beyond e-commerce. From the very beginning, he believed that Amazon would become "the everything store"—a place where people could buy anything, anytime. The key to Bezos's success? Patience. While other startups focused on short-term wins, Bezos played the long game. He reinvested profits back into the company, focused on customer experience, and slowly but surely, Amazon grew into the behemoth it is today. Passionate? Absolutely. Pragmatic? You bet.

Conclusion: Vision Before Everything

At the end of the day, **vision** is what separates a successful startup from the ones that fizzle out after a few months. But vision isn't just about dreaming big—it's about knowing how to take those dreams and turn them into reality. That means defining a clear vision, balancing your passion with a healthy dose of pragmatism, and learning from the visionaries who have come before you.

So go ahead, dream big, but don't forget to keep your feet on the ground. After all, the best founders aren't just visionaries—they're visionaries with a plan.

Rule #2: Customer Obsession is Key

In the fast-paced world of startups, customer obsession isn't just a buzzword—it's the foundation of any successful business. As a startup founder, your survival depends on your ability to understand, attract, and retain customers. Being customer-centric means more than just responding to feedback; it's about deeply understanding their needs, behaviors, and pain points. This chapter explores the essentials of customer obsession, from building products people actually want, to understanding your target market, and the critical process of gathering and implementing feedback early.

Building Products People Actually Want

One of the most common mistakes startup founders make is building a product they believe is revolutionary—without validating whether it solves an actual problem for real people. Many founders fall in love with their ideas, sometimes to the point of ignoring their customers' real needs. The difference between a successful startup and a failed one often lies in the founder's ability to align their vision with their customers' demands.

Focus on Solving Problems, Not Building Features

It's easy to get caught up in the excitement of adding new features, but successful startups are those that focus on solving a specific problem first. Customers don't care about how many cool features you have; they care about how your product makes their lives easier. Your product must serve a clear purpose from the start, and the best way to ensure that it does is to start with a problem and reverse-engineer the solution.

Instead of asking, "What cool feature can I add next?" ask, "What problem am I solving for my customers?" When Airbnb started, they didn't set out to create a global hospitality platform. They started by solving a problem—people needed affordable places to stay during conferences. By solving that small, specific problem, Airbnb built the foundation of a massive company.

The Minimum Viable Product (MVP) Approach

The concept of the minimum viable product (MVP) is critical to ensuring that you're building a product people actually want. An MVP is the simplest, most pared-down version of your product that solves a core problem for customers. It allows you to get your idea into customers' hands as quickly as possible and start gathering feedback.

Building an MVP forces you to focus on the core value proposition of your product, and it helps you avoid over-investing time and resources in features that may not even resonate with your audience. A successful MVP doesn't need to be perfect; it needs to be functional enough to solve a problem and start a conversation with customers.

Case Study: Dropbox

When Dropbox first launched, the company didn't invest in creating a fully polished product. Instead, they released a simple video explaining the core concept: syncing files across devices effortlessly. The video captured the attention of early adopters, and thousands signed up for the beta version of the service. Dropbox used this feedback to refine the product before officially launching. By focusing on solving a specific problem and validating that there was a market demand, Dropbox avoided wasting time and resources on unnecessary features and quickly became a household name.

Avoid the "Feature Creep" Trap

Feature creep is one of the most dangerous pitfalls for startups. It occurs when you continually add features to your product, diluting the core experience in an attempt to make everyone happy. While it's tempting to add features that you think might attract more users, this often leads to a bloated product that confuses and frustrates your core audience.

To avoid feature creep, return to the fundamental question: does this feature solve a problem for my target customers? If the answer is no, it's best to save that idea for later.

How to Truly Understand Your Target Market

Knowing your market inside and out is one of the most important things you can do as a startup founder. If you don't understand your customers' behaviors, motivations, and pain points, you'll struggle to build a product that resonates with them.

Customer Personas: A Snapshot of Your Ideal Users

Creating detailed customer personas is a great way to keep your team focused on who you're building for. A persona is a fictional representation of your ideal customer based on market research and real data about your audience. Each persona should represent a specific segment of your target market and should include key details such as:

- Demographics (age, gender, location, etc.)
- Job role or lifestyle
- Pain points and challenges
- Goals and motivations
- Buying habits or decision-making process

Customer personas help ensure that every decision you make is aligned with the people you're trying to serve. These personas aren't set in stone—your understanding of your customers will evolve over time, and your personas should evolve with them.

Market Research: Gathering Data from Your Audience

Understanding your target market requires both quantitative and qualitative research. You need to gather data that tells you who your customers are, what they want, and how they behave.

Quantitative research, such as surveys or data analytics, provides numerical insights that help you identify trends and measure customer behaviors at scale. Tools like Google Analytics or social media analytics are essential for tracking how people are engaging with your product and where potential opportunities lie.

Qualitative research, on the other hand, focuses on deeper insights and understanding the "why" behind customer behavior. This type of research typically includes interviews, focus groups, or observational studies. Qualitative research is incredibly powerful for discovering the pain points, motivations, and emotional drivers that influence your customers.

Competitor Analysis: Learning from the Landscape

No startup exists in a vacuum. Competitor analysis helps you understand what's already working (or not working) in your industry. Analyze the products, services, and strategies of other companies to identify gaps in the market or opportunities for differentiation.

Some questions to ask during a competitor analysis include:

- What problems do their products solve?
- What do customers love or hate about their offerings?
- How do they market to their audience, and what strategies seem to resonate?

While you should never directly copy a competitor, understanding their strengths and weaknesses can give you valuable insights into what might resonate with your own customers. You can also identify opportunities to innovate where they are falling short.

Emotional Intelligence: The Secret to True Connection

Understanding your market requires more than just hard data; it requires emotional intelligence. Emotional intelligence allows you to connect with your customers on a deeper level, fostering loyalty and trust. It's about recognizing their unspoken needs, reading between the lines of their feedback, and empathizing with their frustrations.

Startups that prioritize emotional intelligence build stronger customer relationships because they're not just solving technical problems—they're addressing emotional ones too. When you truly understand your customers' pain points, you're able to create products that don't just meet their functional needs but resonate with them on a personal level.

Gathering and Implementing Feedback Early

Listening to your customers is one of the best ways to refine your product and ensure that you're on the right track. Gathering feedback early and often is critical to building something that truly works for your audience.

Why Early Feedback Matters

Many startup founders wait too long to start gathering feedback. They focus on perfecting the product before releasing it to the public. This approach often leads to wasted time and resources because you're guessing at what your customers want rather than validating your assumptions with real data.

By collecting feedback early, you avoid building a product based on untested assumptions. This allows you to make quick adjustments before you've invested too much into a flawed direction. It also shows your customers that you're listening and valuing their input, which helps build loyalty and trust from the start.

Feedback Channels: How to Get the Insights You Need

There are many ways to gather feedback, from informal conversations with early adopters to structured surveys and interviews. Some of the most effective methods include:

- **User Testing:** Allow early users to interact with your product in a controlled environment while you observe their behavior and reactions. User testing provides valuable insights into how real people use your product and where they might encounter friction.
- **Surveys:** Send out surveys to gather quantitative feedback from a larger group of users. Surveys are great for tracking overall satisfaction, identifying common issues, and gauging interest in new features.
- **In-App Feedback:** Implement tools that allow users to provide feedback directly within your product. This could be a simple rating system, comment box, or more detailed form that users can fill out while using your app or website.
- **Social Media Listening:** Monitor social media platforms for mentions of your product or brand. Customers often share their thoughts, both positive and negative, on social media, and this unfiltered feedback can be incredibly valuable.

The Importance of Actionable Feedback

Not all feedback is created equal. As a founder, you'll need to distinguish between feedback that's actionable and feedback that's merely noise. Some customers will request features or changes that are out of alignment with your vision, while others will provide insights that can drive critical improvements. The key is to find patterns in the feedback you receive and prioritize changes that will have the greatest impact on your customers' experience.

For example, if multiple users are struggling with the same feature, it's a sign that something needs to be adjusted. On the other hand, if one customer requests a niche feature that doesn't align with your product's overall direction, it's okay to set that aside for now.

Case Study: Slack

When Slack first launched, the team relied heavily on early user feedback to shape the product. Slack's founders were incredibly responsive to their users, constantly tweaking the app based on feedback from teams who were using it. By staying deeply connected to their early adopters, Slack was able to create a product that perfectly met the needs of its core audience, which contributed to its rapid adoption.

Closing the Loop: Let Customers Know You're Listening

One of the most powerful ways to build loyalty is to show your customers that their feedback has been heard and acted upon. Whenever you implement a suggestion or fix an issue based on feedback, let your users know. This can be as simple as sending a thank-you email or highlighting changes in a product update. By closing the loop, you show customers that their input is valued and that you're committed to making the best possible product for them.

Conclusion

Customer obsession is more than just listening to feedback—it's about building a deep, empathetic understanding of your customers and using that knowledge to create products they genuinely need. By focusing on solving problems, building a deep understanding of your target market, and gathering feedback early, you set the foundation for long-term success. Startups that prioritize their customers from day one are the ones that rise above the competition and build lasting loyalty in an ever-evolving market.

Rule #3: Build a Team, Not a Workforce

The success of a startup is not just about the vision of its founder or the product it delivers; it's about the people who bring that vision to life. One of the most important roles of a modern startup founder is to cultivate a strong, cohesive team rather than simply hiring a workforce. This chapter will explore how recruiting passionate talent, fostering a strong company culture, and embracing the power of diversity can transform a startup from a struggling venture into a thriving enterprise.

Recruiting Passionate Talent

Finding the right people for your startup is more than just checking off qualifications and skills on a résumé. While technical expertise is important, passion is what drives teams to push through the challenges unique to startups, from limited resources to the uncertainty of early growth. A workforce may show up for a paycheck, but a team that's deeply passionate about the company's mission will go the extra mile when things get tough.

1. Why Passion Matters in Startups

Startups operate in environments where roles are fluid, challenges are constant, and every person's contribution can have a significant impact on the company's trajectory. Passionate employees are intrinsically motivated—they believe in the mission and are personally invested in the company's success. This level of engagement is especially crucial during early-stage development, where financial rewards may be limited, but the promise of building something meaningful is a powerful driver.

Imagine an early-stage startup struggling to bring a new tech product to market. A talented engineer might know how to code the product, but if they lack passion, they might not care enough to iterate and improve upon it when bugs arise. A passionate engineer, on the other hand, will find creative solutions, stay up late fixing problems, and contribute beyond the basic expectations.

For startup founders, it's essential to identify this passion during the recruitment process. One common mistake is hiring based purely on résumé credentials. While experience and skills are important, passion is often a better predictor of long-term success. Look for candidates who show genuine enthusiasm for your mission. Ask them why they want to join your company specifically, not just any startup. Look for indicators that they're excited by the challenge, not just by the prospect of a job.

2. Crafting a Recruitment Process that Attracts Passionate Talent

The recruitment process should reflect your company's values and culture. The typical corporate hiring approach won't work for startups because you're not just filling roles—you're shaping the future of your company. Start by ensuring that your job descriptions clearly convey your startup's mission and vision. Avoid the sterile, jargon-heavy listings common in the corporate world. Instead, share your story and explain why your startup exists. Let potential candidates feel the heart of your company from the first interaction.

When interviewing candidates, focus on questions that reveal their intrinsic motivations. Ask about challenges they've overcome, projects they've worked on outside of their formal roles, and what aspects of your mission resonate with them. Look for passion in their responses, not just technical proficiency.

It's also worth considering unconventional hires. Sometimes, passion and potential outweigh formal experience. A candidate who doesn't meet all the technical requirements but has shown initiative, creativity, and a drive to learn may bring more value in the long term than someone with a perfect résumé but no genuine interest in your product.

3. Building a Reputation as a Passionate Startup

Passionate talent is drawn to passionate companies. Your startup's reputation plays a significant role in attracting the right people. Invest in building an authentic brand that showcases your company's mission, values, and vision. Social media, blog posts, and interviews can help communicate what makes your startup special. Highlight the impact your company is aiming to make in the world and why your team loves working there.

Attracting passionate talent is a long-term strategy. The more you build a brand around your values, the easier it will be to draw like-minded individuals. Consider how companies like Patagonia or SpaceX have successfully built reputations for being mission-driven. Employees want to work there because they align with the company's greater purpose.

Fostering a Strong Company Culture

Once you've recruited passionate talent, your job is far from over. A passionate team needs a strong company culture to thrive. Culture is the backbone of any successful startup, providing a shared set of values, beliefs, and practices that bind the team together. It's what makes your company unique and is essential for maintaining morale, engagement, and alignment, particularly during challenging times.

1. Defining Your Startup's Culture

At the heart of company culture is purpose. Your startup's mission isn't just something you share with investors or customers—it's what motivates your team every day. A purpose-driven culture ensures that everyone understands the "why" behind their work, creating a sense of belonging and shared responsibility. Employees should feel that they're contributing to something larger than themselves.

Defining culture starts with the founder. Your values, principles, and attitudes shape the company from day one. Are you a founder who prioritizes innovation over bureaucracy? Are you focused on employee well-being and work-life balance? Whatever your values are, they must be clearly communicated and reinforced daily.

Culture also involves the behaviors and norms that develop organically within the team. Whether it's informal team lunches, collaborative problem-solving sessions, or a commitment to transparency, these practices build trust and connection. In the early stages of your startup, these behaviors might develop naturally, but as your company grows, it's important to formalize and nurture them.

2. Creating an Inclusive Environment

Inclusivity is a key aspect of a strong company culture. Startups are often dynamic and fast-paced, which can unintentionally alienate individuals who don't fit a stereotypical mold. Fostering an inclusive environment means actively working to ensure that everyone feels valued and has a voice. This can be achieved through open communication channels, clear feedback mechanisms, and efforts to include all perspectives in decision-making.

Leaders should model inclusivity. If a founder demonstrates openness to diverse ideas and actively seeks input from all team members, it sets the tone for the rest of the organization. An inclusive culture not only leads to higher employee satisfaction but also promotes creativity and innovation.

3. Celebrating Wins and Embracing Failures

Startups are full of highs and lows. How a team celebrates successes and handles setbacks plays a huge role in shaping company culture. Regularly celebrating small wins keeps morale high and reminds the team that they're making progress, even when things feel uncertain. Recognize achievements publicly, whether it's hitting a milestone, solving a complex problem, or even closing a small deal. This doesn't have to be elaborate—sometimes a simple shout-out in a team meeting is enough.

On the flip side, creating a culture that embraces failure is equally important. In startups, failure is inevitable. The key is ensuring that failure becomes a learning experience rather than something to be feared. Encourage your team to experiment, take risks, and share their lessons openly. When team members feel safe to fail, they are more likely to innovate and push boundaries, which is crucial for startup growth.

The Power of Diversity in Teams

Diversity is more than just a buzzword—it's a strategic advantage. Diverse teams bring a wealth of perspectives, experiences, and ideas that can drive innovation, creativity, and problem-solving. In the startup world, where agility and adaptability are crucial, diversity can be the difference between stagnation and growth.

1. Why Diversity is Critical to Startup Success

Startups are solving problems that often require out-of-the-box thinking. A homogenous team, while easy to manage, may fall into groupthink and miss key opportunities or fail to see potential risks. Diverse teams, on the other hand, bring a variety of perspectives that can challenge assumptions and lead to more innovative solutions.

Diversity goes beyond visible traits like gender, race, or age—it also includes diversity of thought, background, and experience. A team member with a different cultural background might see a market opportunity that others overlook. Someone with a non-traditional career path might offer a fresh approach to problem-solving.

For example, consider the case of Airbnb. When the founders were struggling to gain traction, they brought in advisors and employees with different perspectives who helped them identify key user behaviors and optimize the platform. By embracing diverse viewpoints, Airbnb was able to refine its business model and become a global success.

2. Building a Diverse Startup Team

Building a diverse team starts with intentional recruitment. Founders must actively seek out candidates from different backgrounds and experiences. This means widening your recruitment pool, eliminating biases in the hiring process, and creating an environment where diverse candidates feel welcome and valued.

One way to do this is by partnering with organizations that specialize in promoting diversity in tech and startups. Additionally, rethinking your hiring criteria can help attract more diverse candidates. For instance, instead of focusing solely on résumés, consider how candidates' life experiences or problem-solving approaches might contribute to your team.

During interviews, ensure that you're not unconsciously gravitating toward people who remind you of yourself. Startup founders often fall into the trap of hiring individuals with similar traits or backgrounds because it feels familiar and safe. However, challenging yourself to hire people who think differently will create a richer, more dynamic team.

3. The Impact of Diversity on Company Culture

A diverse team enhances company culture by introducing new ideas, perspectives, and ways of working. This leads to more robust problem-solving and creativity, which is vital in the fast-paced world of startups. Moreover, diverse teams tend to be more adaptable and resilient, as they are used to navigating different viewpoints and challenges.

Diversity also fosters inclusivity, as team members who come from different backgrounds are more likely to create a culture of openness and respect. In turn, this culture attracts even more diverse talent, creating a virtuous cycle of innovation and inclusivity.

Conclusion

Building a team, not just a workforce, is one of the most critical rules for modern startup founders. Recruiting passionate talent ensures that your team is invested in the company's mission, fostering a strong company culture unites the team and creates a sense of purpose, and embracing the power of diversity unlocks new ideas and perspectives that drive innovation.

By following Rule #3, you are laying the foundation for a dynamic, resilient team that can navigate the unique challenges of the startup world. As a founder, your team is your greatest asset—treat them as such, and they will propel your vision forward.

Rule #4: Fail Fast, Learn Faster

In the world of startups, failure is inevitable—but it's also one of your greatest assets. The "fail fast, learn faster" principle is not just about experiencing setbacks; it's about learning from them rapidly and using those lessons to move forward more intelligently. This chapter explores the importance of failure in the growth process, how you can leverage failure as a learning tool, and strategies to ensure you're always learning faster than you're failing.

Embracing Failure as Part of Growth

One of the hardest truths for any startup founder to accept is that failure is not just a possibility; it is an essential part of the journey. In fact, most successful founders wear their failures like a badge of honor, because they know it's these stumbles that have shaped their success. But how do you go from fearing failure to embracing it?

Failure is Not the End—It's a Teacher

Many founders enter the startup space with grand visions of success, but few understand that failure is not only inevitable—it is vital. The road to a successful startup is paved with mistakes, dead-ends, and pivots. The quicker you learn to accept this reality, the more equipped you are to turn those failures into valuable lessons. Consider Thomas Edison's famous quote about inventing the lightbulb: "I have not failed. I've just found 10,000 ways that won't work." This mindset is essential for founders.

Instead of focusing on the emotional burden of failure—such as feelings of inadequacy or regret—shift your mindset to see it as an educational experience. Each failure is an opportunity to gather data, analyze it, and move forward with a deeper understanding of your market, your product, and yourself.

Reframing Failure

The secret to embracing failure lies in reframing it. It's not a measure of your personal worth, and it's not an indictment of your vision. It's simply feedback. In startup culture, there's a reason why phrases like "failing forward" have become so popular. The key difference between successful founders and those who give up is how they react to failure. Rather than seeing it as a brick wall, they see it as a stepping stone.

Founders must normalize conversations about failure. The fear of failure can be paralyzing if it's not addressed openly. If you and your team are afraid to take risks because you're worried about the consequences of failure, innovation will stall. But when failure is viewed as part of the process, it becomes much easier to take bold steps and think outside the box.

The Dangers of Avoiding Failure

Many startups fail not because of bad ideas, but because of the founder's unwillingness to take risks and accept potential failure. When founders play it safe, they often fail in a much bigger way—they run out of money or lose market relevance because they didn't take the necessary risks early on. Avoiding failure might feel comfortable in the short term, but in the long term, it will stifle growth and innovation.

As a startup founder, it's crucial to embrace failure as an opportunity for growth. Whether it's a product feature that flopped or a marketing strategy that didn't land, each failure gives you the opportunity to refine your approach. The faster you fail, the faster you learn—and the quicker you can course-correct.

Lean Methodologies

One of the most effective ways to incorporate failure into your startup's DNA is through the use of lean methodologies. These frameworks are designed to minimize waste while maximizing learning, making them perfect for startups that need to fail fast and learn faster.

What is Lean Methodology?

Lean methodology, popularized by Eric Ries in **The Lean Startup**, revolves around creating a Minimum Viable Product (MVP) and gathering feedback as quickly as possible. The idea is to develop the simplest version of your product—one that delivers enough value to be useful—without pouring resources into features or aspects that haven't been validated yet. Once the MVP is launched, feedback is gathered and used to make incremental improvements.

The philosophy behind lean is simple: why spend months or years developing a product only to find out no one wants it? By focusing on delivering just enough functionality to test your core assumptions, you reduce the risk of major, expensive failures and can pivot quickly if needed.

Failing Small and Failing Often

Lean methodology encourages frequent, small failures rather than one massive, catastrophic failure. By testing assumptions early with an MVP, you're setting yourself up for continuous feedback loops. These small failures help you avoid much larger ones later down the road. Each iteration of your product gives you more data, more customer insights, and more opportunities to adapt before it's too late.

Startups that adopt lean methodologies often find themselves more agile and better able to weather market changes or customer demand shifts. They aren't tied to a particular product or strategy—they're constantly learning and evolving.

Build, Measure, Learn Cycle

At the heart of lean methodology is the ***Build-Measure-Learn*** cycle. This process helps startups refine their ideas, test them in the market, and then make improvements based on real-world data. Here's how it works:

- **Build**: Create an MVP of your product. The focus should be on quick deployment rather than perfection.
- **Measure**: Gather data on how customers are interacting with your MVP. What do they like? What do they ignore? What causes confusion?
- **Learn**: Analyze the feedback and decide whether to pivot (change direction) or persevere (continue improving the product).

This process should be repeated until the product and market fit perfectly, but the speed of the cycle is critical. The quicker you can run through this cycle, the faster you can learn from your failures.

Iteration Cycles

Iteration is the essence of failing fast. In a startup, the only constant is change. You have to be willing to throw out assumptions, pivot, and iterate constantly. Iteration cycles help you learn from failure in real-time and allow you to make continuous improvements.

What is an Iteration Cycle?

An iteration cycle is simply the process of refining and improving your product through continuous development, testing, and feedback. Each iteration is a step toward a more polished and market-ready product. Iteration cycles can range from a few days to a few weeks, depending on the complexity of the product and the feedback you're gathering.

Unlike traditional product development, where you spend months or even years creating a final product, iteration cycles involve launching smaller, incomplete versions of your product in stages. Each version is tested, feedback is gathered, and improvements are made. Then the cycle starts again.

The Benefits of Rapid Iteration

Rapid iteration allows you to test your assumptions quickly and make changes before you invest too much time or money into a product that might fail. Instead of waiting until a product is fully built to find out if it's viable, iteration allows you to course-correct as you go.

For example, if you launch an MVP with three core features and one feature is completely ignored by users, you can quickly remove or rework that feature before it drains more resources. On the other hand, if users gravitate toward a feature you hadn't expected, you can double down on its development.

Rapid iteration also makes your team more resilient to failure. When you're working in smaller, more frequent cycles, failures become less significant because you can address them immediately. This fosters a culture of innovation and learning rather than one of fear and hesitation.

Iteration in Action

Imagine you're building a task management app. Instead of spending a year developing every possible feature you think users might want, you launch with just the basics: creating and assigning tasks. Within weeks, you learn that users don't care about assigning tasks—they're using the app solely for personal task management. Instead of stubbornly sticking to your initial plan, you pivot, focusing on a simplified personal to-do list app. This pivot might save you months of development time on features no one wanted.

By learning to iterate quickly and often, you stay aligned with your users' needs and minimize waste in both time and resources.

Case Studies of Startups that Learned from Failure

Some of the biggest names in tech have one thing in common: they've all faced significant failures. However, what sets them apart is their ability to learn from those failures and iterate rapidly.

Case Study 1: Slack

Before Slack became the giant workplace communication tool that it is today, it was an online gaming company called Tiny Speck. The team behind Slack spent years developing a massively multiplayer online game called *Glitch*, which failed to gain traction. Despite their best efforts, *Glitch* was not a commercial success, and Tiny Speck eventually shut down the game.

But the team learned a critical lesson: the internal communication tools they had developed to manage the game's creation were incredibly effective. Instead of letting the failure of *Glitch* define them, they pivoted, repurposing the communication software into what we now know as Slack. Within a few years, Slack became one of the fastest-growing startups in history.

Slack's ability to fail fast and learn faster was pivotal to its success. They didn't dwell on the game's failure—they took the valuable lessons from that experience and applied them to a new product that fit a much bigger market need.

Case Study 2: Instagram

Instagram started as a location-based social media app called *Burbn*. The app allowed users to check in at specific locations, make plans for future meetups, and share photos. However, the app was overly complicated, and users weren't engaging with most of its features.

The founders, Kevin Systrom and Mike Krieger, realized that users were mostly using the app to post photos and apply filters. Rather than stubbornly trying to force users to engage with the other features, they scrapped the entire app, except for the photo-sharing element, and rebranded as Instagram. The simplified app took off, and within two years, it was acquired by Facebook for $1 billion.

Instagram's story is a classic example of the power of iteration. By failing fast with **Burbn** and focusing on the feature users actually wanted, they were able to pivot into one of the most successful social media platforms ever created.

Case Study 3: Airbnb

In its early days, Airbnb was far from the billion-dollar company it is today. The founders struggled to get people to use their platform and even resorted to selling boxes of cereal during the 2008 presidential election to raise money. The company faced multiple rejections from investors, who didn't believe the idea of renting air mattresses to strangers would take off.

However, Airbnb's founders believed in their vision and learned quickly from their early failures. They began to iterate on their initial model, improving the website's design, tweaking the business model, and gathering more feedback from both hosts and travelers. Eventually, their persistence paid off, and they scaled into a global platform that changed the way people travel.

Conclusion: Turning Failure into Your Startup's Greatest Asset

The journey of a startup founder is fraught with failure, but it's not failure itself that determines your success—it's how you respond to it. By embracing failure as an essential part of growth, adopting lean methodologies, iterating rapidly, and learning from the failures of others, you can build a more resilient, adaptable, and successful startup.

The faster you fail, the quicker you learn, and the stronger your startup becomes. Failure isn't the enemy—it's your greatest teacher.

Rule #5 – Master the Art of Networking

Introduction: Networking is Everything

The startup world is not just built on great ideas, visionary leaders, or innovative products—it's built on connections. In the modern startup ecosystem, who you know can often be just as important as what you know. Successful founders understand that their network is one of their most valuable assets. Networking is about creating and maintaining mutually beneficial relationships, tapping into resources, and gaining access to opportunities that can propel your startup forward. Whether you're looking for investors, team members, customers, or advice, mastering the art of networking is essential to success.

In this chapter, we'll explore how to build strategic relationships, find mentors and advisors, and leverage networking to secure funding.

Building Strategic Relationships

At its core, networking is about relationships—genuine, authentic connections that are mutually beneficial. Strategic relationships go beyond casual acquaintances; they are purposeful partnerships that align with your startup's mission and long-term goals.

1. The Power of Reciprocity

One of the most important principles of building strategic relationships is reciprocity. Networking is not just about what others can do for you, but also what you can bring to the table. When you provide value to someone else—whether through advice, connections, or resources—you build goodwill and trust. Founders who approach networking with a "give first" mentality often find that opportunities flow back to them in unexpected ways.

For example, consider offering to connect someone with an expert in your network, provide feedback on a product, or share a useful resource. These small gestures can lead to bigger opportunities, as the people you help are likely to reciprocate when you need assistance.

2. Aligning with Shared Values and Goals

Strategic relationships are most effective when both parties have shared values and complementary goals. As a startup founder, it's crucial to build relationships with individuals who understand and support your vision. Whether it's potential business partners, advisors, or key team members, aligning on core principles ensures a smoother collaboration and a more productive relationship.

When seeking out strategic relationships, look for people who share your passion for the problem you're solving or the industry you're disrupting. This common ground creates a strong foundation for collaboration.

3. Nurturing Relationships Over Time

Building strategic relationships is not a one-time effort—it requires consistent engagement. Like any relationship, business connections need nurturing. This doesn't mean constantly asking for favors but rather maintaining open communication, sharing updates, and staying on each other's radar.

Founders should invest time in checking in with their network, attending industry events, and even grabbing coffee or hopping on Zoom for casual conversations. A relationship built over time is more likely to endure and pay dividends when opportunities arise. Remember, networking isn't transactional—it's about long-term relationship building.

4. Diversifying Your Network

A common mistake startup founders make is focusing only on industry-specific networking. While it's important to have a strong presence in your industry, your network should also be diverse, encompassing professionals from different fields and backgrounds. A diverse network broadens your perspective, introduces you to new ideas, and provides access to resources you might not find in your immediate circle.

For example, a founder in the tech space might benefit from relationships with marketers, designers, legal experts, and even social impact leaders. These diverse perspectives can help you navigate challenges, approach problems creatively, and tap into different markets.

Finding Mentors and Advisors

One of the most valuable aspects of networking is finding mentors and advisors who can guide you through the startup journey. These individuals often have years of experience, deep industry knowledge, and insights that can help you avoid common pitfalls.

1. The Importance of Mentorship

Mentorship is a critical asset for any startup founder. A mentor can offer you a unique perspective that's grounded in experience, helping you navigate the uncertainties and challenges of scaling a business. The key is to find a mentor who aligns with your vision and has experience relevant to your stage of growth.

The best mentors aren't just there to give advice—they challenge you, provide accountability, and help you make more informed decisions. They become your sounding board, offering honest feedback that can help you course-correct early.

When searching for a mentor, look for someone who has been where you want to go. If you're in the early stages, find a mentor who has successfully taken a company from idea to product launch. If you're scaling, seek out someone with experience growing a business from 10 to 100 employees or securing Series A funding. The right mentor will help you focus on the right challenges at the right time.

2. How to Approach Potential Mentors

Building a mentor-mentee relationship doesn't happen overnight. It requires a thoughtful and respectful approach. Start by identifying individuals whose experiences and values align with your goals. Then, begin engaging with them organically—this might mean attending a talk they're giving, reaching out on LinkedIn with a personalized message, or asking for a brief informational interview.

When approaching potential mentors, be clear about what you're seeking. Instead of asking, "Will you be my mentor?" start by asking for specific advice or feedback on a problem you're facing. This allows the relationship to develop naturally over time. Once a rapport is established, you can transition to a more formal mentorship structure.

Remember, mentors are busy people, so be respectful of their time. Come to every conversation prepared, with clear questions or challenges you'd like to discuss. This shows that you value their time and are serious about learning.

3. Turning Mentors into Advisors

As your relationship with a mentor deepens, there may come a point where it makes sense to bring them on as an official advisor. Advisors often take a more active role in your startup, offering ongoing guidance, attending board meetings, and even helping you make high-stakes decisions. In return, advisors typically receive equity in the company, though the exact arrangement varies.

When bringing a mentor into an advisory role, be transparent about your expectations and the level of involvement you need. Whether you're looking for someone to guide your product development, help you prepare for fundraising, or offer strategic advice on scaling, make sure both parties are aligned on the advisor's role and commitment.

Advisors can also open doors to their networks, introducing you to investors, customers, or other key players. The right advisor can have a transformative impact on your startup's trajectory.

The Role of Networking in Securing Funding

For many startups, securing funding is one of the most critical—and challenging—steps in the journey. Networking plays a crucial role in connecting founders with investors, whether through angel investors, venture capitalists, or crowdfunding platforms.

1. Why Investors Invest in Relationships

Investors aren't just investing in ideas—they're investing in people. A strong network can be the key to getting your foot in the door with the right investors. Many early-stage investors, particularly angel investors, prefer to invest in founders they know or who come highly recommended by someone in their network.

That's why warm introductions are so powerful. A personal recommendation from a trusted connection carries much more weight than a cold email. Networking enables you to build these connections, positioning you for introductions to potential investors.

It's important to remember that investors look for founders they can trust. Your ability to build and maintain relationships is a strong indicator of your leadership potential. Investors want to know that you can manage partnerships, work well with your team, and maintain good relationships with customers.

2. Leveraging Networking Events and Pitch Competitions

Attending startup networking events, industry conferences, and pitch competitions can be an effective way to meet investors. These events bring together entrepreneurs and investors, creating opportunities for in-person interactions that can lead to future funding.

When attending these events, come prepared with a clear and concise elevator pitch that communicates the value of your startup. Focus on what makes your product or service unique, the problem you're solving, and why now is the right time for your business. Investors meet countless entrepreneurs, so it's essential to make a memorable impression.

In addition to formal events, informal meetups, dinners, and even coffee chats can lead to valuable introductions. Don't underestimate the power of casual conversations—some of the best connections are made in low-pressure environments.

3. Building Long-Term Investor Relationships

Securing funding is not a one-time transaction; it's the beginning of a long-term relationship with your investors. It's essential to treat this relationship as a partnership. Keep your investors updated on your progress, be transparent about challenges, and involve them in key decisions when appropriate.

Founders who build strong relationships with their investors often find it easier to secure follow-on funding down the road. Additionally, investors who believe in your long-term vision can become advocates, introducing you to other investors or strategic partners who can help you scale.

It's also worth noting that not all investors are created equal. Look for investors who not only bring capital to the table but also have experience in your industry, connections in your market, or a track record of supporting startups at your stage. The right investor can offer strategic advice and open doors that propel your business forward.

4. Crowdfunding as a Networking Opportunity

For founders looking to avoid traditional VC routes, crowdfunding can be a powerful alternative. Platforms like Kickstarter, Indiegogo, and Republic allow startups to raise funds directly from their network, as well as from a broader audience of potential customers and backers.

Crowdfunding is not just about raising money—it's a networking opportunity. Each backer becomes an advocate for your brand, spreading the word about your product and introducing you to new potential customers or partners. Successful crowdfunding campaigns often generate significant buzz, attracting media attention and even the interest of institutional investors.

To maximize your crowdfunding campaign, leverage your existing network for initial support and create a strong marketing strategy that encourages backers to share your campaign with their own networks. The viral potential of crowdfunding can help you expand your reach far beyond your immediate circle.

Conclusion: Networking as a Lifelong Skill

Networking isn't just a phase in your startup journey—it's a lifelong skill that will continue to serve you throughout your career as a founder. Building and maintaining strong, authentic relationships is the foundation of success in the startup world. Whether you're seeking strategic partners, mentors, or investors, the relationships you cultivate will open doors, provide guidance, and create opportunities that can propel your business to new heights.

By mastering the art of networking, you'll position yourself as a leader in your industry, capable of navigating the complexities of the startup ecosystem with confidence and clarity.

Rule #6: Be Financially Savvy

The ability to manage finances is a defining skill for any startup founder. In the early stages, your company's financial health can determine its survival. Every successful founder knows how to manage cash flow, understand burn rate, weigh the pros and cons of bootstrapping, and navigate the murky waters of securing investments from seed funding to venture capital. In this chapter, we'll delve into these critical areas so you can make informed financial decisions that will support your startup's growth.

Managing Cash Flow and Burn Rate

Cash flow is the lifeblood of a startup. If your company runs out of cash, no amount of ingenuity, customer loyalty, or market demand can save you. As a founder, you need to understand exactly how money moves in and out of your business, and more importantly, how to control it.

The Importance of Cash Flow

Managing cash flow is about more than just tracking expenses and income. It's about understanding when money will be available and planning accordingly. For example, if your customers take 60 days to pay invoices but your bills are due every 30 days, you'll experience a cash crunch. These mismatches in timing are what kill many startups, not a lack of revenue or potential.

Think of your cash flow like the air you breathe—it's invisible, yet its absence is deadly. Many startups fail because they overestimate how long they can survive without a steady inflow of cash. Managing cash flow effectively will allow you to:

- Cover operational costs
- Invest in growth initiatives
- Respond to emergencies or unexpected expenses

The Role of Burn Rate

Burn rate, or the speed at which your company spends money, is another critical metric to track. Every startup burns through cash before turning a profit, but it's the pace of that spending that often makes or breaks the company. Burn rate is typically broken into two categories:

1. **Gross burn rate:** The total amount of money your startup spends each month.

2. **Net burn rate:** How much money you're losing each month after revenue is factored in.

To calculate your burn rate:

$$\text{Burn rate} = \frac{\text{Initial Cash Reserve}}{\text{Monthly Operating Expenses}}$$

This tells you how long your cash reserves will last under current conditions.

Founders must be relentless in controlling burn rate to avoid running out of money too soon. Hiring too quickly, taking on too much office space, or overspending on marketing campaigns are common mistakes. A sustainable burn rate gives you more time to test, iterate, and find product-market fit.

Scenario: The Burn Rate Dilemma Imagine your startup raises $500,000 in a seed round. Your monthly expenses are $100,000, leaving you with a five-month runway (your runway is how long you have before the money runs out). Without a revenue stream, you'd have to raise more money or drastically cut costs within five months. By keeping your burn rate lower, say at $50,000 a month, you'd have 10 months—doubling your time to find profitability or additional funding.

Bootstrapping vs. Seeking Investment

One of the earliest financial decisions founders face is whether to bootstrap or seek external funding. Both approaches have their merits and challenges, and choosing the right one depends on your business model, risk tolerance, and long-term vision.

The Bootstrapping Route

Bootstrapping means growing your business using your own resources or revenue, without outside investment. While this approach is often slower, it has several advantages:

- **Ownership and Control:** You retain 100% ownership of your company and make all the decisions. There's no need to answer to investors or dilute your equity.
- **Focus on Profitability:** Without investor money, you're forced to find a way to generate revenue early on, which can lead to a more sustainable and grounded business model.
- **Creativity and Resourcefulness:** Operating with limited resources forces you to be more creative and disciplined, honing your ability to prioritize what's essential.

However, bootstrapping comes with significant challenges. Growth may be slower, and scaling can be difficult without external capital. It's a path that often requires deep personal sacrifice, whether that means investing your life savings, taking out personal loans, or working a second job while building your company.

When Bootstrapping Works Best

- You have low initial costs and can quickly generate revenue (e.g., software or service-based businesses).
- You want to maintain full control and ownership over your vision.
- You prefer to grow steadily without the pressure to achieve hypergrowth.

- You have a clear path to profitability without needing significant upfront investment.

Seeking External Investment

On the other hand, seeking external investment—whether from angel investors, venture capitalists (VCs), or crowdfunding—can offer more immediate access to capital, allowing you to scale faster. But with this financial support comes a loss of control and pressure to deliver results.

Pros of External Investment:

- **Fast Growth:** You have more resources to scale quickly, hire talent, and invest in product development and marketing.
- **Network and Mentorship:** Investors often come with valuable industry connections and can provide guidance on strategy and growth.
- **Risk Sharing:** By bringing on investors, you reduce your personal financial risk.

Cons of External Investment:

- **Equity Dilution:** You'll have to give up a percentage of your company, reducing your ownership stake and future earnings potential.
- **Pressure to Scale:** Investors expect high returns, often pushing for aggressive growth that may not align with your vision or the market's needs.
- **Loss of Control:** Investors may demand a seat on your board or exert influence over key business decisions.

Scenario: The Investment Dilemma Imagine you've built a promising SaaS platform and have bootstrapped it for the first year. You're generating revenue but need $1 million to accelerate growth and hire developers. Bootstrapping further would mean slow progress and limited marketing, while accepting a VC offer for $1 million requires giving up 20% of your company. Which path aligns with your long-term goals?

Navigating Seed Funding, Angel Investors, and VCs

Securing funding is a complex process that involves understanding the different types of investors and funding rounds. Each has its nuances, benefits, and challenges. Let's explore the options.

Seed Funding

Seed funding is typically the first official round of capital raised for a startup. This funding helps get your business off the ground, pay initial employees, and develop your product to a point where it can attract further investment.

Seed rounds are often relatively small, ranging from $100,000 to $2 million, depending on the industry and the region. Seed investors are usually more focused on the potential of your idea and team than on current revenues or profit margins. They know you're at the beginning of your journey and are betting on your ability to execute.

Types of Seed Investors:

- **Friends and Family:** Often, the very first round of funding comes from your personal network. These investors are betting on you, rather than your idea, and typically have fewer expectations of fast returns.
- **Angel Investors:** Angels are individuals who invest their own money in startups. They often come from entrepreneurial backgrounds and may offer mentorship along with funding.
- **Micro VCs:** These are small venture capital firms that focus on seed-stage companies. They tend to offer less capital than traditional VCs but are more accessible to early-stage founders.

Angel Investors

Angel investors play a crucial role in the early stages of a startup's life. These individuals typically invest between $25,000 and $100,000 per deal, though some high-net-worth angels may invest much more.

Angels are often less risk-averse than institutional investors and are willing to invest in unproven business models or founders with limited experience. In return, they typically seek equity or convertible debt, meaning their investment will convert into shares of the company at a later stage.

What Angels Look For:

- A compelling and scalable idea.
- A talented, passionate founding team.
- Some evidence of market demand, even if it's early-stage traction.

Many angel investors are motivated by more than just financial returns. They enjoy being part of the startup ecosystem and mentoring new entrepreneurs.

Venture Capital (VC)

Venture capital firms are professional investment organizations that pool money from limited partners (LPs) to invest in startups. VCs usually come into play during later funding rounds (Series A, B, C, etc.) when your startup has demonstrated significant traction and growth potential.

Unlike angel investors, VCs tend to invest larger sums of money—often starting at $2 million and going into the hundreds of millions for successful companies. In exchange, they expect equity and often push for a substantial say in company decisions.

What VCs Look For:

- Rapidly growing revenue streams or significant user growth.
- A scalable business model.
- A strong, experienced team with the ability to execute.
- A clear path to a large market and eventual profitability.

VC firms usually invest with the expectation of an exit within 5-10 years, either through an acquisition or an IPO. This pressure can shape the direction of your company, often pushing you toward aggressive growth strategies.

Navigating Investor Expectations

When you take money from investors, you're not just gaining financial resources—you're also taking on their expectations. Investors want to see a return on their money, and this can add pressure to scale, grow, and eventually exit.

Here's how you can navigate these expectations:

- **Set realistic milestones:** From the start, align with your investors on what success looks like. Create a roadmap with clear, attainable milestones.
- **Communicate openly:** Keep your investors in the loop with regular updates, whether you're hitting your targets or facing challenges. Transparency builds trust.
- **Balance growth with sustainability:** While investors often push for rapid growth, you should prioritize the long-term health of your company. Scaling too fast can lead to operational inefficiencies, poor customer experiences, or even burnout within your team.

Conclusion: Financial Savvy is Non-Negotiable

Becoming financially savvy is not just a "nice to have" skill for modern startup founders—it's a necessity. The ability to manage cash flow, keep burn rate under control, and make smart decisions about bootstrapping versus seeking investment will give you the financial runway you need to succeed.

Equally important is understanding the landscape of seed funding, angel investors, and VCs so that you can find the right financial partners who align with your vision. Above all, financial savvy allows you to maintain control, execute your plan, and build a startup that stands the test of time.

By mastering Rule #6, you'll ensure that your company is not just surviving, but thriving—financially and strategically.

Rule #7 – Innovate Relentlessly

Innovation is the lifeblood of every modern startup. In a world that moves at lightning speed, staying static is the quickest way to irrelevance. As a founder, you're not just tasked with coming up with one great idea—you need to create a culture of innovation that continuously drives your company forward. This chapter will explore how to foster a culture of continuous innovation, how to stay ahead in a fiercely competitive market, and showcase some of the most innovative startups that are leading the way today.

How to Foster Continuous Innovation

1. Start with the Right Mindset
Innovation isn't just about technological breakthroughs or groundbreaking products—it's a mindset. It requires thinking beyond conventional solutions and a relentless drive to make things better. As a startup founder, you must embody and champion this mindset throughout your company.

One of the most important things to instill in your team is that innovation doesn't only happen at the leadership level. Anyone—from an intern to a senior developer—can contribute groundbreaking ideas. Encourage your team to question assumptions, challenge the status quo, and think outside the box.

Creating a culture that nurtures this kind of thinking starts with how you respond to ideas. If employees fear criticism or rejection, they'll be less likely to take creative risks. Recognize that not every idea will be a hit, but every idea has the potential to inspire something better. Celebrate attempts at innovation—even when they fail.

2. Encourage Cross-Disciplinary Collaboration
The most innovative ideas often come from unexpected places. By encouraging collaboration across different departments, you'll unlock fresh perspectives that wouldn't have surfaced otherwise. For instance, a product designer and a marketer working together might come up with a customer-focused innovation that neither would have thought of on their own.

Break down silos within your organization and create opportunities for cross-functional teams to work together. This could be through hackathons, brainstorming sessions, or even simple weekly meetings where different departments share their latest challenges and insights.

A famous example of cross-disciplinary innovation is Apple's original iPhone team, which included experts in software, hardware, and design. Together, they created a product that revolutionized the smartphone industry.

3. Allocate Time and Resources to Innovation

Many founders claim to value innovation, but few back it up with the necessary time and resources. Innovation needs space to thrive—whether that's giving your team time to experiment or providing them with the tools they need to test new ideas.

Google's famous "20% time" policy is an excellent example of this. The policy allows employees to spend 20% of their time working on side projects that aren't necessarily related to their primary job. This approach has led to the creation of some of Google's most successful products, including Gmail and Google News.

As a startup founder, you might not have the luxury of implementing a 20% time policy, but you can still allocate regular "innovation time" for your team. Even dedicating one day a month for the team to focus on creative exploration can lead to incredible breakthroughs.

4. Encourage Iteration, Not Perfection

Innovation is rarely perfect the first time around. Often, it's the result of multiple iterations—small changes that lead to significant improvements over time. This is why fostering a mindset of iteration, rather than perfection, is crucial.

Encourage your team to get comfortable with releasing "good enough" versions of their ideas, and then iterating based on real-world feedback. This is a key principle of the Lean Startup methodology—build, measure, learn. By getting your product in front of users early, you'll have valuable data to guide future innovations.

Remember, perfection is the enemy of progress. The goal is to get your ideas out into the world and continuously refine them.

Staying Ahead in a Competitive Market

1. Keep a Finger on the Pulse of Your Industry
In a competitive market, staying ahead means knowing what's happening around you at all times. Keeping track of industry trends, technological advancements, and even your competitors' moves is essential for staying innovative.

However, it's not enough to just follow the trends—you need to anticipate where the industry is heading. As Wayne Gretzky famously said, "I skate to where the puck is going to be, not where it has been." This proactive approach allows you to stay one step ahead of the competition.

Set up systems to monitor trends and gather insights from your industry. This could be through attending conferences, reading industry reports, networking with other founders, or even subscribing to relevant news outlets and podcasts. Your goal is to stay informed and understand how shifts in the industry could impact your business.

2. Adapt Quickly to Market Feedback
Successful startups don't just innovate in a vacuum—they listen to their customers and adapt accordingly. This is especially important in a competitive market, where customer needs and preferences can change rapidly.

A great example of this is Netflix, which originally started as a DVD rental service. As streaming technology advanced and customer preferences shifted, Netflix quickly pivoted to become the leading streaming service we know today. Their ability to adapt to market trends and customer needs allowed them to outpace competitors like Blockbuster, which failed to innovate.

Stay in constant communication with your customers, gathering feedback and insights that can inform your next moves. Whether it's through surveys, user testing, or social media, your customers are your best source of information for staying competitive.

3. Invest in Emerging Technologies

One of the most effective ways to stay ahead of the competition is by leveraging emerging technologies before they become mainstream. By being an early adopter, you'll have a head start over competitors who are slower to embrace new tools.

For example, startups that embraced artificial intelligence (AI) and machine learning (ML) early on were able to develop products that outperformed those relying on traditional algorithms. This gave them a competitive edge in industries like healthcare, finance, and e-commerce.

However, don't just invest in technology for the sake of it. Ensure that any new technology you adopt aligns with your long-term vision and solves a real problem for your customers. Blindly following tech trends can lead to wasted resources and failed products.

4. Foster a Culture of Curiosity

Staying ahead in a competitive market requires constant learning. Encourage a culture of curiosity within your team, where employees are not only allowed but encouraged to explore new ideas, trends, and technologies.

This might mean providing access to online courses, encouraging attendance at industry events, or simply setting aside time for team members to research and learn about new developments. By fostering a learning environment, you'll ensure that your team is always equipped with the latest knowledge to fuel innovation.

Some of the most successful companies today, like Amazon and Tesla, have fostered cultures of relentless learning and curiosity. Their ability to stay ahead of the competition comes from their commitment to understanding the latest advancements and applying them in innovative ways.

Examples of Startups Leading in Innovation

1. Airbnb: Revolutionizing the Travel Industry
Airbnb is a prime example of how relentless innovation can disrupt an entire industry. Founded in 2008, the company started as a platform for renting out spare rooms in people's homes. Today, it's a global giant in the travel industry, offering unique stays, experiences, and even luxury accommodations.

One of the keys to Airbnb's success has been its ability to continually innovate. They've expanded beyond traditional accommodations by offering "Airbnb Experiences," allowing travelers to book unique local activities, like cooking classes or guided hikes. This innovation has added a new dimension to their platform, setting them apart from competitors like Booking.com and Expedia.

Airbnb's success didn't come from copying existing models—it came from creating a whole new way to travel, driven by a relentless commitment to innovation.

2. SpaceX: Pushing the Boundaries of Space Exploration
SpaceX, founded by Elon Musk, is one of the most innovative companies in the world today. It's not just their groundbreaking technology—such as reusable rockets—that sets them apart, but their relentless drive to push the boundaries of what's possible in space exploration.

One of the key innovations that have fueled SpaceX's success is their focus on reducing the cost of space travel. By developing reusable rockets, they've drastically lowered the cost of launching satellites and spacecraft, making space exploration more accessible.

SpaceX's commitment to continuous innovation is evident in their ambitious plans, such as developing the Starship spacecraft to take humans to Mars. This relentless drive to explore new frontiers is what makes them a leader in their industry.

3. Slack: Transforming Workplace Communication

When Slack first launched, it seemed like just another workplace chat tool. However, through continuous innovation and a deep understanding of user needs, Slack has become an essential tool for teams worldwide, transforming how we communicate at work.

One of Slack's most innovative features is its integration with other tools and apps. By allowing users to bring together all of their workplace tools—such as project management software, CRM systems, and file storage—Slack became much more than just a chat app. It became a central hub for productivity.

Slack's ability to listen to customer feedback and innovate accordingly has allowed them to stay ahead of competitors like Microsoft Teams. Their relentless focus on improving the user experience has made them a leader in workplace communication.

4. Peloton: Reinventing Fitness Through Technology

Peloton, the fitness company known for its connected exercise bikes, has revolutionized the fitness industry through its innovative use of technology. By combining high-quality fitness equipment with live and on-demand workout classes, Peloton has created a unique fitness experience that's accessible from home.

Peloton's innovation didn't stop at bikes—they've expanded into treadmills and offer a diverse range of workout programs, from yoga to strength training. Their ability to integrate fitness, technology, and community has set them apart from traditional fitness brands.

Peloton's success comes from their relentless commitment to innovation, constantly improving their platform, adding new features, and expanding their offerings to meet the evolving needs of their customers.

Conclusion

Innovation is the key to staying relevant, competitive, and successful in today's fast-paced startup ecosystem. As a modern founder, your ability to foster continuous innovation, stay ahead of industry trends, and leverage new technologies will define your success. By creating a culture that embraces creativity, encourages iteration, and adapts to market changes, you'll ensure that your startup doesn't just survive—it thrives.

The examples of Airbnb, SpaceX, Slack, and Peloton demonstrate that innovation isn't a one-time event. It's a mindset and a practice that must be embedded in the very fabric of your company. Whether you're developing new products, exploring new markets, or improving existing processes, your commitment to relentless innovation will be the driving force behind your success as a startup founder.

Rule #8 - Adapt or Die

Adaptability has become one of the most critical traits of modern startup founders. In a world where industries are constantly disrupted by new technologies, market trends, and shifting consumer preferences, only those who can pivot and evolve stand a chance of survival. Startups, more than established businesses, are in a position to be agile, and this agility is often the key to thriving in a rapidly changing world.

This chapter explores why adaptability is crucial for survival and success. We'll delve into how to navigate market shifts and trends, pivot without losing your core identity, and draw lessons from successful startups that embraced change.

Navigating Market Shifts and Trends

The pace of change in today's market can feel overwhelming. Technologies that didn't exist a decade ago—like AI-driven automation, blockchain, or the gig economy—are now driving forces behind multiple industries. As a startup founder, your ability to see these changes coming and respond swiftly will define your longevity.

Understanding Market Shifts

A market shift refers to significant changes in how industries operate, driven by external forces like technological advancements, changes in consumer behavior, regulatory changes, or economic conditions. These shifts often alter how businesses deliver products and services, how customers perceive value, and what they expect from brands.

- **Technology:** Advancements in technology have disrupted industries from retail to transportation. Think about how the ride-sharing industry disrupted traditional taxi services, or how cloud computing reshaped software distribution.
- **Regulation:** Changes in regulations can open up opportunities for startups or pose new challenges. For example, the legalization of cannabis in certain regions has given birth to a new industry, while GDPR regulations around data privacy have forced tech startups to re-evaluate their business models.
- **Consumer behavior:** Market shifts also arise from changing consumer behaviors. The move toward sustainability has spurred a wave of eco-friendly startups. A growing preference for convenience and digital solutions has accelerated the rise of on-demand services.

Tracking Trends

Being adaptable isn't just about responding to shifts that have already happened. It's about identifying trends early and positioning your startup to take advantage of them. This requires a deep understanding of your industry and the broader market.

Here are some strategies for staying on top of market trends:

- **Industry Reports:** Regularly reading industry reports from research firms like McKinsey, Gartner, and Forrester can give you insight into emerging technologies and market forecasts.
- **Competitor Analysis:** Keeping an eye on your competitors can show you where the industry is headed. If several of your competitors are experimenting with new technologies or adjusting their business models, that's a signal that the market is shifting.
- **Consumer Feedback:** Your customers are often the best source of information about market trends. Pay attention to their needs, complaints, and desires. Conduct regular surveys or use social listening tools to identify patterns in customer feedback.
- **Conferences and Networking Events:** Attending industry conferences and networking events keeps you connected with others in your space. These are often the first places where new trends are discussed and disseminated.

Responding to Market Shifts

Once you've identified a market shift, the next step is to develop a strategy to respond to it.

- **Proactive Adaptation:** When you anticipate a change coming, begin integrating it into your long-term strategy. For instance, if you see that consumers are moving toward a subscription model, you might explore how your product or service could fit into that model before your competitors do.

- **Reactive Adaptation:** Sometimes, a market shift catches you by surprise. In these cases, it's essential to respond quickly without panicking. Evaluate the impact on your business, consult with your team, and make strategic adjustments. While a reactive approach may feel more urgent, it's important to maintain a level head to avoid making rash decisions.

Pivoting Without Losing Your Core Identity

The term "pivot" has become almost synonymous with the startup journey. Some of the most successful companies in the world started as something completely different before they made a significant shift in their business model, product offering, or market approach. But pivoting is more than just changing direction; it's about making strategic adjustments without losing sight of your startup's essence.

What is a Pivot?

A pivot occurs when a company changes its business strategy or model to meet new demands, overcome challenges, or take advantage of a new opportunity. The pivot is often seen as a dramatic shift, but it doesn't always have to be. It can involve changing the target market, altering the product, or even shifting the entire business model.

However, a successful pivot isn't about starting from scratch. It's about using the knowledge, assets, and strengths you've already built while adapting to a new path.

When Should You Pivot?

Knowing when to pivot is one of the hardest decisions a founder will face. The signs are not always obvious, and the process can feel like admitting defeat. However, pivoting at the right time can be the difference between failure and success.

Here are some signs that it might be time to pivot:

- **Stagnant Growth:** If your startup has reached a plateau where revenue and user growth have stalled despite your best efforts, it may be time to consider a pivot.
- **Market Mismatch:** If you realize that your product or service isn't resonating with your target market, despite your

initial assumptions, a pivot could help realign your offering to meet market demand.
- **New Opportunities:** Sometimes, a pivot comes from recognizing a better opportunity. For instance, Instagram started as a location-based check-in app but pivoted into a photo-sharing platform when they realized the popularity of photo-sharing features.

How to Pivot Without Losing Your Identity

The challenge with pivoting is to do so without losing the core identity of your company—the values, mission, and vision that inspired you to start the business in the first place. Here are some steps to make sure your pivot retains your essence:

- **Revisit Your Vision and Mission:** Before making any significant change, revisit your original vision and mission statement. Does the pivot align with your broader purpose? Are you staying true to the problem you set out to solve? These guiding principles should act as your North Star during the pivot.
- **Leverage Your Strengths:** Pivoting doesn't mean throwing everything out. Identify what has worked for your startup so far. Maybe your team excels in customer service, or your technology is innovative. Use these strengths to fuel the next phase of your business.
- **Communicate Transparently:** Whether it's to your customers, team, or investors, be transparent about the reasons behind the pivot. Explain how this change will allow the business to serve them better or tap into new opportunities. This will help maintain trust and alignment throughout the process.
- **Experiment First:** Instead of diving headfirst into a pivot, consider running small experiments to validate the new direction. A pivot doesn't need to happen overnight—it can evolve as you gather more data and insights.

Lessons from Startups That Adapted Successfully

Many of the most successful startups today wouldn't exist in their current form if they hadn't adapted along the way. Let's explore some well-known examples of companies that pivoted and adapted to market shifts, ultimately setting themselves up for success.

Slack: From Gaming to Enterprise Software

Slack, one of the most successful communication platforms today, wasn't always focused on team messaging. The company initially started as Tiny Speck, a gaming company that built an online game called Glitch. Despite their efforts, the game failed to gain traction.

However, while building the game, the Tiny Speck team developed an internal messaging tool to communicate more effectively during the development process. After recognizing the potential of the tool, they pivoted the company to focus entirely on it. Today, Slack is a multibillion-dollar enterprise software giant, all because the founders were willing to adapt when their original idea didn't work.

Key Lesson: Sometimes the most valuable part of your startup isn't your product but the tools or systems you build along the way. Stay open to the possibility that your biggest opportunity might be hidden in unexpected places.

Instagram: From Check-In App to Photo-Sharing Platform

Instagram's journey from a check-in app called Burbn to the leading photo-sharing platform in the world is a prime example of how a well-executed pivot can lead to massive success. Burbn was designed to be a location-based check-in app, but the founders soon realized that users were more interested in the photo-sharing feature than anything else. They made the bold decision to pivot entirely into a photo-sharing platform, which quickly gained traction.

Instagram's focus on simplicity, speed, and visual storytelling enabled it to rise above other platforms at the time and become a social media giant.

Key Lesson: Pay attention to user behavior. Sometimes, what your customers are gravitating toward may not align with your original idea, and that's okay. Listen to them, and don't be afraid to refocus your efforts.

Netflix: From DVD Rentals to Streaming Giant

Netflix started as a DVD rental service that allowed users to rent DVDs by mail, with no late fees. However, as the internet evolved and bandwidth speeds increased, the company recognized the potential of digital streaming. In 2007, Netflix pivoted to streaming video content online.

By embracing this market shift early, Netflix was able to capitalize on the growing demand for on-demand content and eventually became the global entertainment powerhouse it is today. The company's continued adaptability, such as creating original content like ***Stranger Things*** and ***The Crown***, has further solidified its position as a market leader.

Key Lesson: Anticipate technological advancements and be prepared to shift your entire business model if necessary. Netflix's success came from their willingness to bet on the future of digital streaming, even when the DVD rental business was still profitable.

Conclusion: Adaptability as a Survival Skill

In the modern startup world, the ability to adapt is essential. Market shifts are inevitable, and trends come and go. The founders who can navigate these changes and pivot when necessary will not only survive but thrive.

Whether it's responding to changing consumer behavior, pivoting your business to find product-market fit, or staying ahead of industry trends, adaptability is a skill you must cultivate as a startup founder. By learning from those who have successfully adapted and embracing change when the time is right, you'll be better equipped to lead your startup to long-term success.

Rule #9 – Keep Your Customers Close

One of the cardinal truths in the world of startups is that no matter how innovative your product, how passionate your team, or how bold your vision, without a loyal customer base, your startup is doomed to fail. Modern startup founders need to focus as much on retaining customers as acquiring new ones. Loyal customers not only drive your revenue—they become ambassadors of your brand, advocates who bring in referrals, provide invaluable feedback, and give you a competitive edge.

In this chapter, we'll explore how to build long-term customer relationships, the importance of customer retention strategies, and how to measure and improve customer satisfaction.

Building Long-Term Customer Relationships

In the chaotic early days of startup life, it's easy to think of customers in terms of transactions—people who pay for your product and service. But this short-term mindset can be detrimental to your startup's longevity. To succeed as a founder, you must focus on fostering deep, long-term relationships with your customers.

1. Understanding the Customer Lifecycle

Every customer has a lifecycle, which typically moves through stages: awareness, acquisition, engagement, retention, and loyalty. Founders need to understand and manage each phase to ensure that the customer relationship matures beyond the first purchase.

- **Awareness:** At this stage, potential customers have just discovered your brand. They may have stumbled across your social media, heard about you through word of mouth, or seen your product in a marketplace.
- **Acquisition:** Here, they've made a decision to try your product or service. This could be through a trial, a freemium model, or making a purchase.

- **Engagement:** This is the period when the customer interacts with your brand after the purchase. Whether it's through onboarding, customer support, or using the product, engagement is the make-or-break stage. Poor engagement leads to churn.
- **Retention:** Now that customers have engaged with your product, the goal is to keep them coming back. The more value they derive from your offering, the more likely they are to stay.
- **Loyalty:** Loyal customers are the gold standard. They not only stay with you but also recommend your product to others. These are your brand ambassadors who will drive organic growth and reduce the cost of acquisition.

To cultivate long-term relationships, founders need to prioritize each stage, investing in creating a seamless and enjoyable experience for customers. A deep understanding of the customer lifecycle ensures you keep customers in your orbit, moving them from mere buyers to advocates.

2. Personalization is Key

In today's crowded marketplace, customers expect to feel seen and heard. One of the most effective ways to foster long-term relationships is through personalization. With modern tools, founders can collect data on their customers' preferences, behaviors, and needs, and use this information to tailor their interactions.

- **Personalized Marketing:** Gone are the days of one-size-fits-all campaigns. Use customer data to create targeted messaging that speaks directly to their needs. If a customer regularly purchases certain products, send them personalized recommendations or early access to related offerings.
- **Customized Onboarding:** Onboarding should never be generic. Cater your approach to each customer's use case, industry, or business size. Personalized onboarding

experiences increase the chances of customers sticking around longer and using your product more effectively.
- **Individualized Support:** Customer support is a powerful way to build relationships. A fast, empathetic, and personalized response can turn a dissatisfied customer into a loyal one. If a customer feels like you understand their unique challenges, they're more likely to continue doing business with you.

3. Delivering Consistent Value

Building long-term relationships comes down to one fundamental principle: value. Are you consistently providing value to your customers? Whether it's through product updates, customer service, or exclusive content, your customers should always feel like they're getting more than what they paid for.

- **Continuous Product Improvement:** Customers want to know that you're investing in the product they love. Frequent updates, feature additions, and bug fixes are essential to showing that you care about their experience.
- **Educational Content:** Offering valuable content—like webinars, tutorials, or blog posts—gives customers more ways to extract value from your product. It also establishes your company as an industry leader, building trust and long-term loyalty.

Customer Retention Strategies

Customer retention isn't just about keeping people from leaving—it's about creating a deep emotional connection with your brand that makes them want to stay. In many ways, acquiring a new customer is far more expensive than retaining an existing one. With the right strategies, you can keep your customers coming back for more, thus ensuring sustainable growth.

1. The Power of Subscription Models

Subscription models have become one of the most popular ways to encourage customer retention. They provide a predictable revenue stream and naturally encourage repeat interactions with your product or service. This model works particularly well for software-as-a-service (SaaS) startups, but can also be applied in other industries such as subscription boxes, media, and even food delivery.

The key to making subscription models work is providing ongoing value that customers simply can't live without. Think about platforms like Netflix or Dropbox. The recurring charge is worth it because the value provided consistently exceeds the cost. To excel in this area, founders need to continually innovate and ensure that the product's utility is always top-of-mind for the customer.

2. Loyalty Programs and Rewards

Creating a loyalty program can incentivize your customers to stay engaged with your product. Whether it's a points-based system, rewards for frequent purchases, or special perks for long-term customers, loyalty programs create an additional layer of connection between the customer and your brand.

- **Gamification:** Many startups have begun implementing gamification into their loyalty programs, encouraging customers to hit certain milestones and "level up." This not only drives engagement but also taps into the psychology of achievement, making the customer feel like they're progressing alongside your product.
- **Referral Rewards:** Referrals are one of the most powerful tools in customer retention. By incentivizing current customers to bring in new ones, you create a cycle of growth that leverages your existing customer base.

3. Proactive Customer Support

Waiting for customers to come to you with problems is reactive. The best startup founders take a proactive approach to customer support, anticipating needs before they arise. This includes:

- **Regular Check-ins:** Set up automated check-ins with customers to see how they're using your product. Are they getting the most out of it? Do they need help with specific features?
- **Onboarding Programs:** Instead of leaving customers to figure things out on their own, set up a robust onboarding process that walks them through the product, ensuring they see the value right away.
- **In-App Guidance:** Many SaaS products now include in-app guidance systems or chatbots that can help users navigate features without having to reach out for support. This creates a seamless experience that reduces friction and frustration.

4. Exclusive Content and Community

People love feeling like they're part of something exclusive. Offering early access to new features, behind-the-scenes content, or membership in an elite customer group can build strong emotional connections to your brand.

- **Beta Testing Groups:** Letting loyal customers beta test new features before they go live can make them feel valued. They become invested in the success of your product and are more likely to stick around.
- **Creating a Community:** Building a community around your product allows customers to connect with each other, share tips, and offer feedback. These communities can exist on platforms like Slack, Discord, or private forums, and give customers a sense of belonging. It's also an excellent opportunity for founders to engage directly with their customers.

Measuring and Improving Customer Satisfaction

You can't improve what you don't measure. Keeping your customers close requires continuous evaluation of how they feel about your product, services, and brand. By collecting the right metrics and feedback, you can identify areas of improvement and take actionable steps to increase customer satisfaction.

1. Key Metrics to Track

Founders need to track a few key metrics to ensure their customer satisfaction levels are where they should be:

- **Net Promoter Score (NPS):** One of the simplest ways to measure customer satisfaction is through NPS. This asks customers a single question: "How likely are you to recommend our product to a friend or colleague?" Customers respond on a scale from 0 to 10, with higher scores indicating greater satisfaction and loyalty. This metric is valuable because it directly correlates to customer retention and referrals.
- **Customer Satisfaction Score (CSAT):** CSAT is another straightforward way to gauge satisfaction. After an interaction with your product, you can ask customers to rate their experience on a scale of 1 to 5. This quick survey helps identify potential pain points that could affect retention.
- **Churn Rate:** While churn measures how many customers leave, it's an important signal of customer dissatisfaction. Keeping your churn rate low means you're doing something right. If churn is high, it's a red flag that something in your product or service isn't meeting expectations.
- **Customer Lifetime Value (CLV):** CLV measures the total revenue a customer is expected to bring over the lifetime of their relationship with your company. A high CLV means that customers are sticking around and continuing to engage with your product. Tracking CLV can help you identify which customers are your most valuable and what strategies are working best to keep them.

2. Gathering Qualitative Feedback

Beyond quantitative metrics, qualitative feedback is invaluable. You can gather this through:

- **Customer Interviews:** Speak directly with your customers to understand their pain points and where your product can improve. These conversations often reveal insights that you can't gather from metrics alone.
- **Surveys:** Periodically send out more detailed surveys to gauge customer opinions on specific features, the onboarding experience, or support interactions.
- **Focus Groups:** Bringing together a small group of customers to discuss their experience with your product can uncover common issues or desires that you may not have been aware of.

3. Acting on Feedback

The worst thing a startup can do is gather feedback and then do nothing with it. Customers want to feel like their voices are being heard. By acting on their input, you not only improve your product but also build trust with your customer base.

- **Quick Wins:** Look for feedback that can result in immediate changes. This could be something as simple as tweaking a user interface or improving a support process. Quick wins show customers that you're listening and responsive.
- **Product Roadmap Transparency:** If you can't immediately implement feedback, communicate what you're doing and why. Let customers know where their suggestions fit into your roadmap and give them a timeline for future changes.

Conclusion: Keeping Your Customers Close is the Key to Longevity

In the fast-paced world of startups, it's easy to get caught up in the thrill of growth, scaling, and market competition. But as Rule #9 highlights, keeping your customers close is the most effective way to ensure your startup's longevity. Through personalized experiences, proactive customer retention strategies, and continuous evaluation of customer satisfaction, you can build a loyal customer base that not only sustains your startup but helps it thrive for years to come.

The most successful modern founders understand that their customers are more than just buyers—they are the lifeblood of their business, and every interaction counts.

Rule # 10: Lead with Purpose

In the fast-paced, cutthroat world of startups, it's easy to get caught up in the race for growth, funding, and market share. However, amidst the relentless pursuit of success, one critical aspect is often overlooked: purpose. Startups that lead with a clear purpose, a mission beyond profit, and a commitment to social impact are the ones that not only endure but thrive in the long term. Rule #10, *Lead with Purpose*, is about understanding why your startup exists and how to ensure it stays true to its core values.

Defining Your Mission Beyond Profit

Most startup founders begin their journey with a grand vision of changing the world. Somewhere along the way, however, this vision can get overshadowed by the pressure to deliver quarterly results or secure the next round of funding. But a startup driven purely by profit is unlikely to have a lasting impact. Founders who define their mission beyond profit create startups that resonate with customers, investors, and employees on a deeper level.

The Difference Between Vision and Mission

To lead with purpose, you first need to differentiate between *vision* and *mission*. Your vision is the future you want to create — it's the overarching dream that drives you. Your mission, on the other hand, is the specific, tangible impact your startup aims to have on the world. For instance, if your vision is to create a world where sustainable energy is accessible to everyone, your mission might be to develop affordable solar panels for low-income households.

The distinction is important because while your vision can be lofty and aspirational, your mission needs to be actionable and grounded in reality. As a founder, you'll make countless decisions that will shape the direction of your company. Having a clear mission ensures that you stay aligned with your core purpose, even when faced with difficult choices.

How to Craft a Purpose-Driven Mission Statement

Creating a purpose-driven mission statement requires deep reflection on the "why" behind your startup. Ask yourself:

- Why does your company exist?
- What unique problem are you solving?
- How is the world better because of your product or service?

Your mission statement should be concise, specific, and inspiring. It should serve as a constant reminder of why your startup exists beyond making money. Take Ben & Jerry's, for example. Their mission statement goes beyond selling ice cream: ***"to make the best possible ice cream in the nicest possible way."*** This purpose-driven approach has endeared them to customers for decades, reinforcing the idea that companies can succeed by doing good.

Living Your Mission: The Founder's Role

A mission statement is only as powerful as its execution. As a founder, it's your responsibility to ensure that every aspect of your business — from product development to customer service — aligns with your mission. This doesn't just mean talking about your mission in meetings; it means living it every day.

For instance, if your startup is committed to sustainability, you should prioritize eco-friendly practices throughout your operations, even if they cost more. If your mission involves social good, make sure you're giving back to the communities you serve in meaningful ways. Authenticity is key here — today's consumers can easily see through hollow marketing claims. Leading with purpose means consistently acting in accordance with your mission, even when no one is watching.

The Role of Startups in Social Impact

In an era where global challenges such as climate change, inequality, and public health crises dominate the headlines, startups have a unique opportunity to drive meaningful social change. The role of startups in creating social impact goes beyond traditional corporate philanthropy — it's about integrating social good into the very fabric of your business model.

Why Startups are Positioned for Social Impact

Startups have several advantages over established corporations when it comes to driving social impact:

- **Agility:** Startups are typically more nimble and can pivot quickly in response to emerging social needs.
- **Innovation:** By their very nature, startups are designed to solve problems in new and creative ways, making them ideal for addressing complex social challenges.
- **Engagement:** Younger generations of consumers increasingly want to support companies that align with their values. Startups that champion social causes have a built-in advantage when it comes to attracting loyal customers.

In many ways, startups have the power to shape the future by tackling the world's most pressing problems. Founders who understand this role and leverage it strategically will create lasting impact far beyond their immediate product or service.

Embedding Social Impact into Your Business Model

The key to creating a sustainable social impact lies in embedding it into your core business model, rather than treating it as an afterthought. Here are a few approaches:

- **Social Entrepreneurship:** Companies like TOMS and Warby Parker have adopted a "buy one, give one" model,

where for every product sold, they donate to those in need. This approach directly ties their social mission to their business outcomes.
- **Environmental Sustainability:** Many startups are incorporating sustainability into their supply chains, using eco-friendly materials, reducing carbon footprints, and embracing circular economy principles. For example, clothing brand Patagonia is famous for its environmental activism, encouraging customers to buy less and repair more.
- **Empowering Marginalized Communities:** Some startups focus on job creation and economic empowerment for underserved populations. Fair-trade companies, for instance, work directly with artisans in developing countries to provide ethical employment opportunities.

By embedding social good into your business model, you're not only contributing to a better world — you're also differentiating your startup in a crowded marketplace.

The Ripple Effect of Social Impact

When startups take their role in social impact seriously, they create ripple effects that extend far beyond their immediate sphere of influence. Consider how fintech startups have revolutionized financial inclusion by providing access to banking services for underserved communities. Or how health tech startups are improving access to affordable healthcare solutions in developing regions.

The ripple effect doesn't just benefit those directly impacted by your product or service; it also attracts like-minded employees, partners, and investors who want to be part of something bigger. Today, impact investing is on the rise, with investors actively seeking out startups that can deliver both financial returns and social good.

Measuring and Communicating Your Impact

If you're leading with purpose, it's important to measure and communicate your impact transparently. Investors, customers, and employees all want to see the real-world effects of your mission. Tools like B Corp certification, impact assessments, and ESG (Environmental, Social, Governance) metrics can help you quantify your social impact. Just as you track financial metrics like revenue and growth, social impact should be part of your regular reporting.

Remember, however, that social impact isn't about perfection. As a startup founder, you may face trade-offs between profitability and purpose. What matters is your commitment to the long-term pursuit of positive change.

Why Purpose-Driven Companies Outlast the Rest

In today's business landscape, purpose-driven companies aren't just a trend — they're here to stay. The reason is simple: companies that operate with a clear sense of purpose have a competitive edge that sets them apart from profit-driven competitors. This edge translates into long-term resilience, stronger customer loyalty, and an engaged workforce. Here's why purpose-driven companies outlast the rest:

1. Stronger Customer Loyalty

Customers today are more conscious about where they spend their money. They want to support companies whose values align with their own. Purpose-driven brands tap into this by building deep emotional connections with their audiences. These connections go beyond product features and price points — they're about shared beliefs.

Consider the case of Patagonia. The company's commitment to environmental activism has cultivated a fiercely loyal customer base that isn't just buying outdoor gear; they're buying into a movement. As a result, Patagonia has been able to command premium prices, maintain strong margins, and sustain its growth over decades.

Startups that lead with purpose create brand advocates who stick around for the long haul, even when competitors offer similar products at lower prices.

2. Resilience in Tough Times

Purpose-driven companies are more resilient in the face of adversity. When you have a clear mission that transcends profit, you can weather challenges like economic downturns, market disruptions, and shifts in consumer behavior more effectively.

Take Ben & Jerry's as an example. Even during economic downturns, the company has stayed true to its social mission of promoting progressive values and social justice. This commitment has helped them maintain a loyal customer base and stay relevant, even when other companies are struggling.

Purpose provides a guiding light during difficult times, allowing companies to make decisions that align with their values rather than short-term financial gains. This long-term focus ensures that purpose-driven companies are built to last.

3. Higher Employee Engagement and Retention

Startups with a strong sense of purpose tend to attract and retain top talent more effectively than those focused solely on profit. Employees want to feel like their work has meaning beyond just earning a paycheck. When they're part of a purpose-driven company, they're more likely to be engaged, motivated, and committed to the company's success.

For example, employees at companies like Tesla or SpaceX aren't just there to build electric cars or rockets — they're there to be part of something transformative, to contribute to a vision of a sustainable future or space exploration. This sense of purpose fosters a deeper connection to the company, resulting in lower turnover rates and a more committed workforce.

4. Attracting Values-Aligned Investors

Purpose-driven startups also attract investors who are interested in more than just financial returns. Impact investors, in particular, are looking for startups that can deliver both profit and purpose. These investors understand that companies with a clear sense of purpose are more likely to build sustainable, long-term value.

In fact, many venture capitalists today are specifically looking for startups that integrate social impact into their business models. For example, firms like DBL Partners and Kapor Capital have pioneered the concept of "double bottom line" investing, which prioritizes both financial returns and positive social or environmental impact. These firms recognize that purpose-driven companies not only have the potential to generate profit but also to address pressing global challenges, making them more resilient and adaptable in the long run.

Values-aligned investors are also more likely to offer patient capital, understanding that meaningful change often takes time to materialize. This allows startups to focus on scaling their social or environmental impact without the pressure of delivering short-term gains. Moreover, these investors often bring valuable networks and expertise in areas like sustainability, social justice, and community engagement, which can help startups navigate the complexities of building a purpose-driven business.

By attracting such investors, purpose-driven startups gain access to both capital and strategic support that aligns with their mission, helping them grow in a way that stays true to their values.

Conclusion: Leading with Purpose for Long-Term Success

As we conclude this book and this final chapter, the message is clear: leading with purpose is not a soft strategy—it's a smart one. The modern startup founder must think beyond the traditional metrics of success. Profit is essential, yes, but it's not the only measure of a company's worth. The companies that will thrive in the future are those that define their mission, contribute to social good, and stay committed to a purpose that transcends financial gain.

By leading with purpose, you'll not only build a business that stands out in the marketplace, but you'll also create a legacy that makes a real, lasting impact. Purpose is what transforms a startup from a fleeting idea into a movement—one that can inspire change, foster loyalty, and drive sustainable success for years to come.

In the fast-paced, ever-changing world of startups, the most powerful competitive advantage you can have is a sense of purpose. It will guide you through challenges, attract the right people, and ensure that your company has a meaningful place in the world.

Lead with purpose, and the rest will follow.

www.ingramcontent.com/pod-product-compliance
Lightning Source LLC
Chambersburg PA
CBHW050329230526
45471CB00005B/2412